Rocket Recall!

Unleash Your Dog's Desire To Return To You Through Motivation-Based Training

Predation Substitute Training™ – Volume 2

Second Edition

Simone Mueller

Contributions by Lhanna Dickson and
Charlotte Garner
Illustrations by Päivi Kokko

Rocket Recall! Unleash Your Dog's Desire to Return to you through Motivation-Based Training has provided the most accurate information possible. The techniques and training protocols used in this manual are state-of-the-art among science-based, force-free dog trainers and behaviourists who specialise in Predation Substitute Training. The author shall not be held liable for any damages resulting from use of this book.

Impressum:
Simone Mueller
Pattbergstrasse 15
74867 Neunkirchen
Germany

Table of Contents

Introduction

Do you dream about having a dog who comes eagerly running back to you when they're called?

Do you feel embarrassed when your dog forces you to scream, shout, and dash after them in public, all while they're gleefully running away from you?

Are you frustrated or worried that the moment something interesting catches their eye, they'll leave you in the dust with no hope of catching them?

Having a reliable "Rocket" Recall ready to go is one of the biggest challenges for dog owners, but it's also the most important "life insurance" you can train into your dog.

Believe it or not, a Rocket Recall can become a reality for you - even if you think there's no way your dog will ever obey. Every dog, no matter what their past behaviours may have been, can learn to come joyfully and reliably when they are called.

It all starts with following the easy step-by-step instructions you'll find in this training program; soon, you'll see the real-life results of a Rocket Recall in your dog, whether they are a young puppy or grown adult dog - simply put, it works!

ROCKET RECALL

Throughout this training program with your dog, you will:

- Learn and use the DOUBLE RECALL, a two-part tool that gives your dog the support that they need to fly back to you, even in the face of his strongest distractions.
- Discover need-oriented and functional reinforcers to reward your dog.
- Learn how to avoid common dog training mistakes that can spoil your success.
- Lock in your dog's Rocket Recall response through fun recall games that range from basic to pro-level.
- Feel empowered to successfully and independently continue training, even long after you have finished this training protocol.

As you begin your journey, remember this important note: the Rocket Recall training program is not about compelling rote obedience from your dog: it's about tapping in to his natural desire to return to you!

I'm itching to get started, and I hope you (and your pup!) are too...

Ready – Steady – Go – Recall!

Part 1: Preparing The Tools You Need

Why Do So Many Dog Owners Struggle With Their Dog's Recall?

A reliable recall is one of the greatest challenges for many dog owners. But why is that so?

First of all, we need to understand that a recall is something aversive - negative - that is happening to the dog. It's something that goes against what they actually want to do in the moment. When we use a recall, we're asking them to turn away and abandon something that they are interested in, or something they want to check out.

Turning away from that interesting smell, person, animal, or other distraction and having to come back to us is the first "disappointment" for the dog. We naturally try to "make up" for this disappointment by giving them a treat, but often, the treat is not really a reward for our dog. Why is this? It's because the treat doesn't fulfill a need that they feel at that moment. Giving a treat is not functional - it's not part of an understood system driven by their instincts - and it can become a second "disappointment" during the recall.

Let's look at it another way, for clarity. Think back and remember the way you felt as a child when a parent called you inside for dinner, but the other kids you were with kept on playing. While you likely enjoyed eating as a normal activity, in this situation, it wasn't what you actually wanted to do. You wanted to remain playing with your friends! You may have even perceived it as a kind of punishment, as you had to leave your friends behind. You felt disappointed, sad, maybe even angry that you had to abandon what you wanted to do, even though it was for something else that you typically enjoyed.

A dog that turns away from chasing a cat, or playing with another dog, might feel the same way, even if we offer them a treat. Even though they love to eat at home and in a non-distracting environment, they might not perceive that same treat as a reward when outside the home. Believe it or not, this is one of the reasons why so many dogs are hesitant or even resistant to taking treats outside.

Exploring the idea of "disappointments" within a recall further, some dog owners struggle with their dog's recall because they consciously or unconsciously punish their dog for coming back. This may look like:

- A prior loss of temper and subsequent yelling at a "naughty" dog that slipped their lead or got out.
- A waver or hardness to your voice, born out of fear that they won't come back the last few steps or may dart into the road.
- Your body language and stance changing to a threatening one when you're preparing to chase them down as they turn away.

Even if you don't remember doing any of these things exactly, human nature dictates you're likely guilty of at least one at some point. It was when this happened that your dog may have started to associate your recall with something negative or punitive - the "disappointment." You recalled your dog from something interesting, put them on lead, or called them away from their friends and ended the fun. According to learning theory, this is punishment.

A final familiar reason why dogs struggle to come back is a lack of training. They may understand what a recall is functionally, in the moment, but not that means recall regardless of the situation. Their owners have trained their recall at home, or in a similar non-distracting environment, but neglected to instil proper generalisation of the cue. In order to generalise the cue properly, you'll need to repeat it hundreds, even thousands, of times in various situations and alongside different distractions.

In order to set our dogs up for success we need to carefully structure these situations and scaffold the distractions, allowing us to work through them in a kind of "bucket list" for our dogs. In this holistic training program, we will tackle all three of the common issues that cause dog owners to struggle with their dog's recall: the reluctance to abandon something interesting, a feeling of punishment, and a lack of training. We'll also learn how to make a reward functional, ensuring it has the intended effect on your dog and doesn't feel like a disappointment.

Throughout this training, you will play pattern games with your dog that rewire their brain, ensuring that coming back to you is no longer a punishment. Once you've properly implemented these techniques, in fact, they'll actually feel the desire to come back to you. We'll also work together to create a well-structured and scaffolded bucket list of distractions, situations and reward options to work through. Let's get started!

Intimidation And Painful Punishment Are Counterproductive!

A trustworthy Rocket Recall is important for a number of reasons. If your dog does not come back when called, it can be embarrassing and difficult for the owner, but it can also leave both dog and owner in danger as well.

Many owners use aversives, such as an e-collar, spray collar or discs in the best interest of the dog, in order to protect them from harm. After all, we all love our dogs and don't want to inflict pain or fear on them. This isn't always the best route, however, for creating the behaviours that you're ultimately hoping for in your dog.

If you use punishment in your dog training, this training program will help you to reduce the use of these aversive tools, eventually abandoning them altogether. So even if you do not train purely positively and prefer a more balanced approach in your dog training, this program may offer new insights and better results.

People tend to get frustrated and angry if their dog ignores their recall. They tend to angrily scream at their dog or scold them, throw a leash or a disc or even use a spray-collar or e-collar. When the dog finally comes back, they grab the dog's collar and push them down in a so-called "alpha roll".

Let me be clear here: the alpha roll and neck shake are NOT suitable ways to punish a dog! They're harmful misconceptions: it's a persistent myth that this is the way that adult dogs punish their puppies. Simply put, alpha rolls and neck shakes do not happen between an adult dog and their offspring. Doing this to your dog may destroy his trust in you, but it will not help them understand your intentions.

When you react aggressively and punish your dog this way for not coming back, you will teach them to avoid you in the future. Eventually, the problem will only get worse: you'll actually be unintentionally training your dog to stay away from you.

So what can you do instead?

To begin with, you'll need to prepare the tools we'll need on your journey to a Rocket Recall!

Your List Of Rewards

What Does Your Dog Love?

When you're attempting to recall your dog, the environment is constantly working against you. Your dog can always reward themself with stimulation in their environment, all while ignoring your cue. This is why it is all the more important to reward a recall with high quality, unique, and need-oriented rewards.

What Can Be A Reward For Your Dog?

The first thing that typically comes to mind when talking about rewards are treats. Treats come in super handy because all dogs need to eat, and treats are easily portable. However, all treats are not the same! Dry kibble, for example, doesn't have the same value as cooked liver. Some dogs love peanut butter, others would do just about anything for a hot dog.

The way you deliver the treat also has a lot of bearing on how he'll like it. Consider your dog's behaviour: does it make a difference if you hand it straight to your dog, or if you toss the treat away from you to catch or chase? Have you tried scattering treats in the grass for them to discover?

What about toys? Does a tennis ball have a different value to your dog than a soft stuffed animal? Would they rather chase a toy or play tug while you hold the other end? Do they find a ball that is thrown rewarding? Would they like it more if you bounced it, or hid it and told them to find it?

Rewards can also come from their environment, in a way that you direct, rather than from their own self-interest. Do they love playing with dogs in the park? Digging in the ground for interesting titbits? Running at the beach? Swimming? Sitting next to you on a park bench while you watch the world go by? Use this a reward!

You can also be the reward yourself! You can pet or massage your dog, praise them with a soft voice, run with them, work with them on their favourite trick, and so on.

Even if your dog doesn't take treats outside, there is a wide array of alternative reward options, such as a tennis ball, a stuffed toy, or even a tug/puller rope toy. If, on the other hand, your dog is super food-motivated, try to be unpredictable with what you offer and surprise your dog with edible treats that feature new flavours and textures.

Take a minute and think about your dog before continuing. Use the form at the end of this training program to make a list of the things – actions, behaviours, treats, etc. – that they love and that you can use as a reward. Don't make it too easy for yourself and write down generic "treats" or "toys", go the extra mile and name specific ones. What kind of treats does your dog find super yummy? Which toy is their favourite? Putting an effort into the following lists will make training easier and more effective for you; we will be revisiting these lists several times during our training journey.

To download the whole training log as a printable PDF from my website, follow the link
http://www.predation-substitute-training.com/rocketrecalltraininglog

Or scan the QR code:

MY DOG NANOOK'S LIST OF REINFORCERS

What does Nanook find rewarding?

Food	Food Delivery	Toys	Environment	Social Interaction
Cat food	Teasing treat	Ball thrown	Swimming	Playing with other dogs
Sausages	Rolling treat	Ball rolling	Digging for mice	Running with me
Cooked liver	Scattering kibble	Playing tug	Sniffing	Cuddling
Meatballs	Licking liver pate	Ball hidden	Fishing treats out of the water	Baby talk
Liver pate		Retrieving toy	Stalking wildlife	Doing a trick
Kibble		Searching prey dummy		

16

Your List of Distractions

What Does Your Dog Find Hard To Disengage From?

A Rocket Recall is one of the most important cues for your dog: it's not just convenient for you, it's also likely to be their life insurance one day. That's exactly why we need to pay attention to carefully building, scaffolding, and training this cue in very small steps.

To create and generalise the Rocket Recall, you first need to understand and recognise what your dog finds hard to leave when you call them back. It's only when you know about these distractions that you can gradually build up their resistance to them, and attention to your recall.

Take a moment and think about your dog again. What do they find hard to leave when you call them back? List the distractions in order of difficulty, from slight to moderate to severe. This is the order that you will later work through! It will be a valuable tool when generalising the Double Recall and its two components, the check-in cue and the anchor cue.

So, you may ask, how do you know whether a distraction is a slight distraction, a moderate distraction or a severe distraction for your dog? Here's how to recognise each stage:

- For slight distractions, your dog can disengage by themself. They look at the trigger briefly, then check-in with you so that you can continue training.
- For moderate distractions, you are still able to recall your dog, but they're communicating

through hesitation or body language that they would still love to go over and check it out.

- For a severe distraction, your recall is a "lost cause." Your dog is off like a bolt of lightning and your recalls are going unheard and unacknowledged.

By arranging your dog's distractions from slight to severe, you are scaffolding the steps on your ladder, ultimately laying the groundwork to a successful and reliable recall. Do not skip or ignore the importance of the steps on this ladder – this will impact your ability to truly implement a Rocket Recall with your dog.

We have mentioned scaffolding a few times in the book so far, but what exactly do we mean? Here's everything you need to know about what scaffolding is, how you can implement it with your dog's recall, and why it's so crucial to developing a solid Rocket Recall:

Scaffolding A Recall

Do you ever feel frustrated that your dog seemingly ignores your recall cue and carries on chasing whatever they have seen? Have you practiced your recall at home loads of times, only for your dog to not respond to it when you are out on walks and really need them to come back?

Often it is the case that your dog's recall doesn't work as well as you would like it to when you find yourself in a highly distractive environment. This could be when the dog is in mid-chase or sees a deer or rabbit for example and their recall fails.

This is likely because this behaviour and cue have not been scaffolded well enough for it to be effective in such a high level of distraction. Not because your dog is ignoring you purposely, or doesn't understand the recall cue itself.

For a recall to be successful in a highly distractive situation, it's vital that you know how to scaffold it effectively.

It's relatively common knowledge now that we need to lay foundations for training new behaviours in non-distractive environments to begin with. So, many people will start teaching their dog their recall basics in their living room, where distractions are very minimal; however, this is often where the progression stops.

A good metaphor to use is to think of your dog's recall like a ladder.

Step 1 on the ladder is practising at home in your living room. Step 2 could be choosing to move training outside into the garden when you are purposely set up for a training session. Then the top step, or Step 10 of the ladder is using your recall in an emergency situation, I.e. when your dog is mid-chase.

However, all the steps and scenarios in the middle of this ladder haven't been worked on and scaffolded effectively. This is often overlooked and the process is rushed through.

However, in order for your recall to function in a 'Step 10 situation,' all of these things need to be properly worked through to create a firm scaffold for the cue and the behaviour. Without this, your recall can't be expected to work or fully relied upon in a Step 10 scenario.

So, you need to keep an eye out for opportunities to practice and scaffold your recall. Each ladder will look different for every individual dog. So, it's a good idea to get a pen and piece of paper and write down what each step would look like for your own dog.

Once you have a clear idea of the types of scenarios you are looking for, you can actively seek these opportunities to practice and scaffold your recall.

Recall is all about disengagement; though this is not always predatory. It could be that you need your dog to disengage and return to you when they see another dog, a child on a swing, a jogger, a cyclist, etc. The aim is to get your dog to choose to disengage and return back to you. When this is scaffolded and practiced effectively, a recall becomes second nature to your dog and an instant reaction for them. However, this can only be achieved when you fully scaffold this cue and behaviour.

Think of the scaffold as a support system for your dog, allowing them to succeed no matter what distractions are happening around them. Without effective scaffolding, the foundations will fall apart and leave you feeling frustrated as your dog disappears into the distance instead of responding to your recall cue!

MY DOG NANOOK'S LIST OF DISTRACTIONS

What does Nanook find hard to disengage from?

severe

- Unfamiliar Dogs
- Running Deer
- Squirrels
- Dog Pee
- Familiar Dogs

medium

- Kids on Skates
- Humans on Bikes
- Joggers
- Mouse Holes

slight

- Food on the Floor
- Leaves on the Ground
- Water

What's The Name Of The Game?

Making Use Of Reward-Specific Markers, Functional Reinforcers And Reinforcement Procedures

Are you excited to connect with your dog and learn how to motivate them to return to you the first time you recall, every time? I'm excited to teach you how! Let's delve into the nitty-gritty of how to reinforce and reward your dog.

Marker Training and Reward Markers

Oftentimes in this book, you will be asked to "mark and reward" a certain behaviour. What does that mean?

Marker training is a science-based teaching method to communicate with your dog what behaviour is desired by you through positive reinforcement.

The so called marker acts as a bridge between the correct behaviour and the delivery of the reward. It is also called a secondary reinforcer.

Whenever your dog has done a behaviour that earns them a reward, you give them your marker signal.

This can be a verbal marker, such as "Yes!" or "Bingo!" or a sound marker, such as a click, produced by a hand-held clicker. The reward marker is always followed by something that the dog loves, such as food, play, cuddles or access to something that they want to have at this moment.

Reward-Specific Markers

A reward-specific marker is a marker that's attached to a specific enjoyable reward.

Think about how you've reinforced recall behaviour up to this point. What reward follows after you have recalled your dog? All too frequently, the dog is rewarded with food. Why is that? Well, food is great as a reinforcer because it is easy for us to carry and most dogs love to eat.

However, rewarding your dog with food alone can and does lead to issues. If your dog has learned that his coming back is always followed by a treat, they will make a choice: Is a cookie what I want at the moment, or do I want to continue doing what I'm doing right now?

Imagine your dog is about to chase a rabbit. You recall your dog and now they have a choice: should I call off the hunt and take that dry cookie? Hmm...I think it's more fun to keep chasing this rabbit!

Link The Act Of Returning To Many Primary Reinforcers

To avoid this predictability, you must reinforce your dog's coming back to more than food, and incorporate a variety of different primary reinforcers.

So what is a primary reinforcer, exactly? A primary reinforcer is anything and everything that makes your dog happy and they'll find enticing in the moment. This does include food, but it also encompasses play, digging, sniffing, social contact, swimming, off-leash time, and so on.

Examples for additional primary reinforcers could include:

- Your dog is heading for a swim? - Recall your dog and send them for a swim as a reward.
- Your dog wants to play with their dog buddy? - Let your dog do a nose touch and interact with their buddy as a reward.
- Ask your dog to keep a "loose leash," then remove the leash as a reward.

Next Step: Name Your Reward!

Now that you have a range of environmental reinforcers available to you, you can now choose some that your dog will love. These "super rewards" now get a name. They become reward-specific markers, which means that your dog connects the name of the reward to what will happen when they hear that name.

One of my dogs, Nanook, loves the reward-specific marker "bowling." When I recall Nanook and he starts to return to me, I'll call out the word "Bowling". When he hears this word, he knows that I will "bowl" a treat along the floor and he is allowed to rush, grab, and eat this treat.

Reward-Specific Markers: The Protocol

The reward-specific marker is first built up in a low-distraction environment. The reward-specific marker must be given first. So, in my case with training Nanook, I would say, loud and clear, "bowling." Only then do I reach into my treat bag, take out the treat and bowl a treat along the floor. In other words:

- Speak the reward-specific name ("Bowling!")
out loud -> wait 1 second -> reach into the bag
-> deliver ("bowl") treat

As with classical conditioning training, this sequence conditions emotions and expectations in the dog along with the cue. Once properly trained in, if your dog hears the cue in the future, this cue alone will trigger the emotions in them that are conditioned with the actual reward: in this case, chasing. Once the dog has learned what the cue means, you can then use it outside as a reward-specific marker to reward the desired behaviour.

The Rewards Specific Marker As A Reinforcer

Your dog sees a rabbit. You recall your dog and while they are running back to you, you call the reward specific marker "Bowling!" Your dog now knows what reward awaits them and knows where that reward awaits them. In my example with Nanook, when he hears the cue "bowling!" he knows, that the action will happen behind him and away from the stimulus. He knows: "Ah, ok, if I now turn away from the rabbit, then I may still chase cookies back there with my human." Now it will be much easier for him to turn away from the rabbit and return to me.

Reward specific markers are an offer to your dog. They tell them, for example, I'm going to roll a cookie back here. If you want and if you can, come to join me and chase the cookie.

If your dog is not able to take advantage of this offer, then it was not the right reward at that moment. Try out a little: What is your dog able to do at which moment? What do they want in this particular situation?

Reinforcers Have To Be Functional

Reward-specific markers aren't simply treats given after a trick - they need a functional element to make a reliable impact on your dog's behaviour. This means that they should come as close as possible to the behaviour your dog actually wants to show, but that you may be interrupting with a recall. For example, if your dog likes to chase things rather than coming back at your recall, bowling is an excellent substitute.

If your dog is more the type that loves to dissect prey, you can wrap up their reward in a paper bag, which you throw in the opposite direction. Use a reward-specific marker like "Shred", so that they know it's okay to grab, dissect the bag, and eat the treat inside.

If your dog is the type that likes to watch prey with their eyes, reward them with "Stalk." Make it clear that they cannot chase the target, but they can watch it as long as they want to.

You can find many more examples of how to reinforce your dog functionally and according to their canine needs in my book "Hunting Together!" – Predation Substitute Training, Volume 1.

Static And Dynamic Reward-Specific Markers

In order to reward your dog according to their needs, you should name both static and dynamic reward-specific markers. Here are a few I use with my dog, to give you some ideas:

Static reward-specific-markers are delivered in a calm way and can be used to calm your dog down.

Some of Nanook's static reward specific markers are:

- **Cookie** – I deliver a treat to his mouth
- **Stalk** – I let him watch the trigger as long as he wants to, all four feet on the floor
- **Search** – I toss treats on the floor or I show him an interesting place to sniff

Dynamic reward-specific-markers are paired with movement and are delivered in a way that builds arousal in the dog.

Some of Nanook's dynamic reward specific markers are:

- **Catch** – I throw a treat that he can catch in the air.
- **Bowl** – I toss a treat across the floor for him to chase.
- **Dig** – I show him a mouse hole or sand pitch.
- **Shred** – I throw him a paper bag or toilet roll with treats inside.

NANOOK'S LIST OF REWARD SPECIFIC MARKERS

What's the action?	Verbal cue
Treat delivered to mouth	Cookie
Watching wildlife – 4 Feet on the ground	Stalk
Throwing treat that that he can catch in the air	Catch
Destroying paper bag or toilet roll	Shred
Showing interesting place to sniff	Go sniff

Reinforcement Procedures For Environmental Reinforcers

Reward-specific markers that make use of reinforcers from the environment are a super powerful tool. This is because you're actually giving your dog the freedom to do what they want to do at this moment. For example, you see your dog's best buddy on the horizon. Before they run over for an excited meet-and-greet, you recall your dog: now, as a reward, you can then send them over to the other dog. They learn that all the good things in their environment come from you.

The problem to be solved is this: does your dog understand that they are being rewarded by you for their recall? To emphasise that the environmental reinforcer is a direct consequence after a recall, you can use reinforcement procedures. Reinforcement procedures are a way of making it clear to the dog that all the good things in the environment come from you and that you provide them as a direct result of showing a certain behaviour.

A good reinforcement procedure works in five steps:

Step 1: Recall your dog.
Put your dog on a leash. Use a basic recall to start the sequence. (Don't worry, the exact protocol of how to build a Rocket Recall will appear later in this training manual.)

Step 2: Name the reward-specific marker that you are going to deliver.
Tell your dog which reward you are about to deliver by naming the reward-specific marker. Start with one behaviour that your dog loves. For example, if you pass a tree on your walk that your dog loves to sniff every time, then condition the reward-specific marker "sniff." Recall

your dog shortly before you arrive at the tree and when your dog looks at you and waits for their reward, say the reward-specific marker "sniff."

Step 3: Start the reward.
When your dog looks at you after you say "sniff," release your dog to their reward by prompting at the tree. Make sure they check-in with you first and does not run to the tree straight away, it must be made clear that the rewards starts with you. If your dog runs to the tree straight away, don't jerk the leash, just patiently hold them back on their harness and wait for them to check-in with you.

Step 4: Stay involved.
While your dog is enjoying their reward, stay involved in the process by praising them and repeatedly naming the behaviour they engage in. Happiness chemicals are naturally flowing through their brain as they enjoy the reward, so you want to be sure to attach your reward-specific markers to this flood of feel-good sensations.

Step 5: End the reward.
If you want to move on, if you realise that your dog is about to lose interest in what they are doing, or if you realise that arousal is about to go through the roof, end the reinforcement procedure. Give an "are you done?" cue, turn away, and praise your dog for following you. If your dog is highly aroused, calm them down with some scattered treats on the ground.

TIP: When you are rewarding your dog, make sure you are upbeat, animated and excited about what they have done. If you show these emotions, it lets your dog know what they have chosen to do is really great!

This is particularly important if you have recalled your dog to you in the presence of wildlife. If your dog is already chasing, or is about to chase a wild animal, they will be excited and wound up by this. If they actively choose to abort the chase and return to you, only to be met with a static, standard reward and half-hearted praise, they will always choose to continue the chase next time; simply because it's much more fun and they are getting what they want at that time by chasing!

Mirroring their emotions cheers your dog on and encourages them to return to you again in the future. It also replicates their feelings of excitement and euphoria, which is potentially being cut short when you ask them to stop chasing wildlife. If they get this response from you, then it's been a worthwhile swap for them to return to you for excitable praise instead of an exciting chase. This turns it into a functional reinforcer for this scenario.

This creates a level of understanding between you and your dog; so always let your happy emotions show!

Part 2: Joint Forces for a Rocket Recall

The Double Recall

What's the Double Recall? Well, it's a combination of Leslie Nelson's "Really Reliable Recall" and Patricia McConnell's finding that short, high and repetitive sounds catch your dog's attention particularly well.

Leslie Nelson's discovery that a recall is a chain of two completely different behaviours, was a game-changer. The key to success is to give the very first behaviour in the chain – the dog's check-in with you and turning away from its trigger - an extremely strong reinforcement history.

In her PhD thesis, Patricia McConnell examined the "Acoustic structure and receiver response in mammalian signal systems" to which acoustic signals mammals react particularly well. She found that traditional animal trainers, such as shepherds, regardless of their language or where they are in the world, use short, rapidly repeated rising notes to speed up their animals and longer, continuous descending notes to slow them down.

The German biologist, dog trainer and behaviourist, Dr. Ute Blaschke-Berthold, combined these two ideas and developed an extremely powerful recall: the Double Recall. The Double Recall consists of two individual parts: the check-in cue, i.e. an extremely thoroughly conditioned positive interrupter and the so-called anchor cue.

"I Just Want My Dog To Come Back When I Call Them!"

It might sound like a simple request but "just coming back" on cue is a complex behaviour and anything but easy. First and foremost is the reorientation of attention, followed by an orientation of the body, movement towards the human and holding attention to the point of contact with the human.

- Reorientation of attention.
- Reorientation of the body.
- Ignoring further distractions.
- Movement towards the human.
- Ignoring further distractions.
- Making contact.

If you look at this in terms of the usual recall training, one thing becomes clear: a single cue for this complex package can open the door to misunderstandings. Let's break down the behaviour into its components and associate it with familiar training elements:

- For reorientation of attention, we need a check-in cue.
- For reorientation of the body, we need a cue for moving towards the human.
- For further movement towards the human, we need to continue the cue for moving towards the human.
- For ignoring further distractions we need a "keep going" signal.
- For making contact we need a reward.

The Check-In Cue – The First Part Of The Double Recall

The Check-In Cue: What It Is

The check-in cue (or reorientation cue) is the integral element of your successful recall. It makes up 90% of your Rocket Recall and requires your most effort. A check-in cue is like a tap on your dog's shoulder: "please leave your canine world for a second and check in with my human world". For your dog, this can be a difficult thing to do!

When chasing prey, your dog might not be able to physically hear your recall anymore. Here's why: hormones, such as Dopamine and Adrenaline, are flooding their body. The thinking part of their brain is shut down and the primal part – the part responsible for basic emotions and instinctive behaviour – is in full control. The only way to interrupt it is to tap into this same part of their brain. This is where classical conditioning (a very strong tool) comes into play.

When we classically condition a check-in cue, we are anchoring it into the part of the dog's brain where emotions happen. When the check-in cue is well-established and sharpened up, therefore, the dog will follow it instinctively - a whiplash reaction.

The Check-In Cue: What It Is Not

Each recall begins with a check-in of the dog. If there is no successful reorientation and check-in, there is no coming back. The dog will continue to focus on their distraction. According to its role, teaching a reorientation signal requires premium training!

People sometimes fail to understand the need for a rocket check-in cue. They want the dog to "just pay attention" to their human, but they forget that a dog lives in their dog world. Every change from dog world to human world is checked by the dog's brain to see if it's needed. Therefore, the environment is the dog owner's biggest competitor.

Without realising it, many people already use a check-in cue before actually recalling their dog. But they aren't always successful. Here are some examples:

- Shouting the dog's name in a threatening and escalating voice if they don't respond.
- Using promising signals (or bribery!) such as waving treats or rustling a bag of goodies.
- Visual stimuli, such as running the opposite way or a hand movement in the dog's field of vision.
- Punishment threatening signals, such as scolding the dog, often in entire sentences that are uttered in a hostile way.
- Aversive impulses that are weak to begin with but become more severe, such as jerking on the leash, running towards the dog or making a hissing noise.
- Noises to intimidate the dog, such as throwing training discs or clapping hands.
- Touch stimuli that become more and more painful, such as jerking the leash, tapping with fingers, using a spray collar or e-collar.

If any of these seem familiar don't worry. Let's, instead, get clear on how to distinguish between a recommendable and less recommendable way to get your dog to check-in with you. All stimuli that lead to a reorientation of the dog (who hasn't been properly conditioned beforehand) are not suitable as reorientation cues. Why? Well, the repetition of such a stimulus leads either to habituation or sensitisation – i.e. the dog either becomes complacent and does not respond to it anymore or they become more and more sensitive. They may even become afraid of the stimulus. Because of these side-effects, check-in cues should be chosen and conditioned carefully.

Isla doing the Check-in Cue.

The Check-In Cue: The Protocol

As a cue, think of a word (no, not your dog's name!) that you don't use too often. "Come" is not a good check-in cue, as we use it constantly when talking to our dogs, e.g. "Fido come here", "Fido come and sit" etc. Setting up several check-in cues is something I would advise too: one with a certain word and one with a whistle. But first, let's work out the best word so we can make it stick. It should be something that you don't feel embarrassed to call out loud and from a distance in a park. Maybe "Puppy!" or "Return" might be an idea.

Step 1: Classical Conditioning
The check-in cue is a so-called positive interrupter. The idea is for your dog to turn their attention back to you and turn to you when they hear the cue, but they do not have to come all the way back!

Try this out at home in a distraction-free environment.

- Make sure your dog is right by your side. We use classical conditioning here, so your dog doesn't have to do anything! We simply pair the cue with a treat.
- Say your check-in cue and immediately give your dog a super high-value treat - even if they don't react to your cue. As long as you are sure they heard you, hand over the treat.
- Repeat five to ten times.

Step 2: Generalisation
Still at home and in a distraction-free environment, wait until your dog is looking away from you and then say your check-in cue. As your dog turns towards you, reward them with a super high-value treat and joyful praise. If you use a clicker or marker signal, this is your click point.

Repeat five to ten times, then pause and do it again four times daily for about ten days inside your house, in different rooms, and using a good mix of high-value rewards from your list.
If your dog reacts to the cue in a whiplash-reaction more than 80% of the time, it's time to up the criteria.

Step 3: Time to take it outside
Look through the list of distractions you made earlier and work your check-in cue through these distractions. Start with the slightest and work through to

the severest distraction. Once you take the check-in cue outside, start to use not only food and toys but also environmental reinforcers from your list of rewards. Keep rewards as need-oriented as possible. If your dog wants to chase, let them chase a treat. If you ask for a check-in while your dog is sniffing the ground, send them back to sniff etc.

For more need-oriented and functional reward options, check out my book "Hunting Together!" - Volume 1 of Predation Substitute Training.

Super-proof your check-in cue for at least a week (four times daily) in various locations outside under increasing distractions and using various high-value rewards. And don't forget to incorporate reinforcement procedures into your training – that's crucial.

Your dog should be successful in more than 80% of the time when they hear the cue. If not, go back one step on your list of distractions.

Important:
- Remember, the check-in cue is not about your dog coming back to you! It's about their initial reaction to the cue - that's what is reinforced. They might turn their head, freeze for a split second or even just twitch their ear. Big or small, every reaction counts.
- Practice the reorientation, not the ongoing attention. As soon as the dog is permanently checking-in into the human world and offering constant eye contact, we end the session.
- Be spontaneous, surprising and unpredictable with your dog, and mix up your high-value rewards from your list of rewards so they never know what to expect.

The Anchor Cue – The Second Part Of The Double Recall

The Anchor Cue: What It Is

The Anchor Cue is a keep going signal that constantly encourages your dog to run back to you and past all the tempting distractions they encounter on their way. The Anchor Cue is repeated until your dog is back by your side. Short consecutive words that can be repeated quickly work best, such as "go, go, go" or "yep, yep, yep". Can you hear how encouraging they sound?

Patricia McConnell found out that shepherds around the world and across languages use short, rapidly repeated tones to speed up their animals.

Isla doing the Anchor Cue.

The Anchor Cue: The Protocol

Step 1: Classical conditioning

Start in an environment with very few distractions. Throw a freebie treat away from you for your dog to run after and eat. It won't take long before they turn around to ask you for more. This is the moment when you start to move backwards, away from your dog and give your anchor cue. While your dog runs towards you, give them your anchor cue until they are by your side. Then, in a bowling movement, throw a treat in the opposite direction and repeat the game. Wait until they finish the treat and turns around. Move backwards and give your anchor cue until they are by your side and then bowl the next treat.

Important: repeat the anchor cue until your dog is by your side!

Play this game five to ten times and make it super fun and exciting for your dog. Try running backwards, shout the anchor cue in an excited voice, and cheer your dog while they run towards the treat. When doing the anchor cue, your dog should be highly aroused and run very fast.

When it's time to wind down, it's important they don't become frustrated. So calm them down by using a less energetic bowl. Give them a treat in their mouth, scatter some treats on the ground and then tell them the game is over.

Tip: Do not make the mistake of repeating your anchor cue too quickly. Later, when your dog will be further away, you'll lose your breath if you don't allow yourself time to pause between the cues. Instead, try to say your cue in the rhythm of your dog's pace. Every time their front paws touch the ground, say your anchor cue.

By conditioning them to gallop in sync with your anchor cue, you will be able to speed your dog up later, if necessary, by accelerating your anchor cue.

Step 2: Generalisation
Play five to ten rounds of this game twice daily for about ten days in various situations outside.

For the anchor cue to function reliably, the rewards must be creative, high-value and varied, as I've previously mentioned. Choose food rewards, toy rewards, and some from the environment. Deliver them with the use of reward specific markers and reinforcement procedures. Now, go back to your list of distractions and work through them again to super-proof your anchor cue.

Tip: If your dog runs back to you spontaneously, it's a good idea to take this as a free opportunity to generalise your anchor cue. Capture the behaviour and match it with the anchor cue.

Putting The Pieces Together: The Double Recall

After having followed and proved the protocol of the check-in and anchor cues, it's now time to put the pieces together. But take it easy. You cannot rush this moment! Wait until you are sure your dog has understood both cues and you would be comfortable betting 100 Euro, Pound or Dollars that they will follow your cue. If you're unsure that they are ready (and you don't want to place any bets yet) go back one step and repeat each protocol individually.

The Double Recall - The Protocol

Step 1: Check-In Cue + Anchor Cue

Start in a low distraction environment. Wait until your dog is a few meters away from you and only slightly distracted. Then give your check-in cue. As soon as they turn around, give your anchor cue and repeat it until your dog is by your side. Reward them with a big treat party or use a super high-value toy to play with them. Repeat five to ten times over the course of one walk.

Step 2: Generalisation

Train the Double Recall indoors and outdoors in various environments. Build up distractions according to your list of distractions and work through them. Use various and high-value reinforcers from your list of rewards and don't forget to apply the reward-specific markers and reinforcement procedures.

As a minimal rule, proof your Double Recall in groups of five:

- In five different environments: house, garden, street, field, woodland etc.
- In five different weather conditions: wind, snow, sunshine, rain, cold etc.
- At five different times: dusk, morning, afternoon, evening, night etc.
- Near five different distractive scents: scent of dog pee, game, sandwich, cat poop, hot dog etc.
- Near five different moving stimuli: kids playing football, bike, jogger, playing dogs, running squirrel etc.

The more diverse, the better! Add in distractions from your list of distractions and arrange them from slight to severe for your dog.

Only up criteria when your dog is successful more than 80% of the time.

To keep track of your training progress, you can download the free Training Log from my website. You can find the link in the back of this book.

What happens when nothing happens? Easy, just go back in the protocol and refresh your recall. This really is a work-in-progress, believe me. It's never finished!

Troubleshooting
Body Language
Dogs are very perceptive. If they see your body language as threatening or hear the merest hint of frustration in your voice they can easily be put off. You have to be mindful of everything. Avoid facing your dog head-on and don't lean forward. Both signal that they must stay away from you. Instead, turn slightly sideways, squat down or walk a few steps backwards and talk to them in a friendly tone.

The 10:1 Rule
Train for the event, not in the event. What does that mean? Well, for each time the Double Recall has a negative consequence for your dog in a real life situation (i.e. leash on, end of the game with their dog buddy, or a recall from that DELICIOUS cat poop!), you should recall them ten times for something great to happen!

Recall your dog from nothing
Do not fall into the trap of only recalling your dog when something happens. They will soon learn that your recall means something exciting is on the horizon and

your recall will become a cue to scan the environment for possible triggers (excitement).

When can I stop rewarding my dog for a recall?
Never! Yes, that's right. Remember that a recall is an aversive event in your dog's life. It interrupts an activity that they really want to engage in, and so to turn away from something so attractive to them and run back to you is an enormous achievement. If you fail to make it worthwhile for them, they will stop following your recall. It's that simple.

In case of emergency
The old rule that a "command is only given once" does not apply for the anchor cue! If your dog runs off, give your check-in cue and then constantly give the anchor cue, even if they keep running away from you or is out of sight. When your dog is in chasing mode, the thinking part of their brain (the part that's responsible for listening to your cue) is switched off and they cannot hear you. Yet, at some point, your dog will need to refocus and orient themself. This is when your anchor cue kicks in and your dog will come back to you.

The Double Recall Using A Whistle

It makes sense to train the Double Recall both with a word cue and a whistle. Why? Well, your dog can hear a whistle from further away than your voice – your word cue. A whistle always sounds the same, no matter if you are hoarse, angry or frustrated. An angry or frustrated tone of voice, as you already know, might put your dog off and is quite embarrassing in public.

The disadvantage of a whistle, though, is that you have to remember to take it with you. So it makes sense to have both tools, word cue and whistle to hand.

The conditioning of a whistle follows the same steps as the conditioning of a word cue. You need to decide on a tone for the check-in cue and a tone for the anchor cue. The check-in cue could be, for example, one long whistle "toooot" or two consecutive short tones "tot-tot" or any other tone you can easily reproduce on your dog whistle. Follow the step-by-step instructions to condition this check-in cue as described in the protocol in section two.

For the anchor cue, it makes sense to use short repetitive whistles in sync with your dog's strides "tot – tot – tot – tot". Again, follow the step-by-step instructions to condition the anchor cue as described previously.

The Double Recall with a whistle is the combination of these two tones: "toooot – tot – tot – tot – tot…".

The step-by-step instructions on how to put the pieces together and successfully generalise the Double Recall will take you through the process of proofing the use of a whistle.

Don't forget to play the following Double Recall Games using the word cue and the whistle.

Part 3: Double Recall Games

The Double Recall Games are variations of the Double Recall. They build a concept in your dog that following your recall rapidly and coming in close to you when being called is the best thing that could ever happen to them. Instead of an aversive event that interrupts their fun, your recall is something your dog looks forward to hearing.

Integrate the following Recall Games into your daily walks and play one or two of them for about one to three minutes daily to see amazing real-life results. Your dog's brain will be hard wired to love to come back to you!

For all the Recall Games, you need some larger, round treats or little meatballs that roll and bounce nicely. This game is about chasing a visual trigger, so the treats should be large enough for your dog to spot them when thrown. If your dog is not food motivated you can also use their favourite toy.

Please have your dog's health checked before engaging in the games and make sure there are no abrupt stops which could hurt their joints.

The following Recall Games are all high arousal games and your dog will love to let off some steam and engage in the physical activity. Don't forget, though, to follow the Curve of Arousal and cool down your dog before you move on.

The Curve Of Arousal

Structuring Dog Training Like A Gym Workout

To be able to compete with stimuli in the environment, your recall and its following reward should always be connected with high arousal in your dog. Arousal is nothing to be afraid of! Everybody needs to let off steam from time to time and our dogs are no exception.

To avoid the frustration of ending the game all too abruptly, it's important to structure your dog training like a workout at the gym.

When a dog is chasing "prey", such as wildlife, cats, tennis balls, or even tossed treats, a cocktail of hormones is released into their body that will strongly influence their level of arousal. Adrenaline and dopamine are pumped into their body, their pain perception is reduced, and their focus is narrowed down.

After the "kill", it takes a while for these hormones to ease. The dog will start to dissect and consume their prey. Just as in many other mammals, the act of chewing and licking has a soothing effect on the dog. Endorphins are released, and the dog calms down.

What does this mean for our reward delivery? Start your play session with a little warm up and gradually build up arousal in your dog. During play time, let your dog be a dog!

You can actively relax your dog after a wild chasing game or a tug-o-war, not by stopping the game abruptly but by gradually lowering the energy, intensity and speed of the game until your dog's body starts to relax. Cool down your dog by fading the dynamic of the flying toy or treat until you finally hand your dog some treats into their mouth and scatter more on the ground. Foraging (i.e. searching the ground for scattered treats) lowers your dog's heart rate and releases endorphins (happy hormones) into the system which calm your dog down. At the end of each play session it's a great idea to scatter treats to avoid your dog becoming frustrated that you stopped the game just when they were having so much fun. Imagine the scattered treats as a cool down after a good workout at the gym.

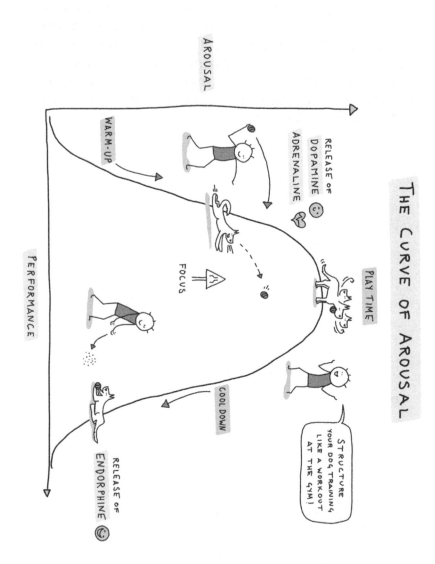

1. The Chase Game – Chasing Treats Instead Of Squirrels

The Chase Game is a game from my book "Hunting Together!" and a part of Predation Substitute Training. You can play it just for fun or as a functional reward if your dog comes back after your recall instead of chasing off. Instead of handing over a dry biscuit, let your dog keep doing what they wanted to do in the first place: chase.

The Protocol:
- Toss your dog a freebie using a bowling movement.
- Wait for your dog to find and eat the treat. The moment they are about to turn around to ask for more, give your check-in cue, followed by your anchor cue.
- Repeat the anchor cue until your dog is with you. Then throw another treat in the opposite direction, so that your dog runs past you.
- Wait for your dog to find and eat the treat. The moment your dog is about to turn around to ask for more, give your check-in cue, followed by your anchor cue again.
- Repeat several times. Bowl the treats back and forth past you five to ten times.
- Don't forget to cool your dog down by fading the energy from your toss, then give a treat from your hand and sprinkle some more treats on the ground before you move on.

Nanook playing the Chase Game.

2. Bowling – Building Acceleration

There are situations in real life when a fast recall can be a lifesaver. The Bowling Game teaches your dog that running towards you at a fast pace is super fun and worthwhile.

Some dogs start their way back fast but slow down on the way back to their guardian. If your dog is turning into a lame duck every time you recall them, check your body language! A threatening body language or a frustrated tone of voice might put your dog off. Avoid standing head-on with the dog or leaning forward.

The Protocol:
- Toss your dog a freebie using a bowling movement.
- Wait for your dog to find and eat the treat. The moment they are about to turn around to ask for more, give your check-in cue and start giving your anchor cue.

- Repeat the anchor cue until your dog is with you. Don't stop your dog but throw the next treat through your legs in the opposite direction, so that your dog runs through your legs.
- Wait for your dog to find and eat the treat. The moment your dog is about to turn around to ask for more, give your check-in cue, followed by your anchor cue again.
- Repeat several times. Bowl the treats back and forth through your legs and let your dog run through your legs five to ten times.
- Don't forget to cool your dog down by fading the energy from your toss, then give a treat from your hand and sprinkle some more treats on the ground before you move on.

Isla Playing the Bowling Game.

For safety: Don't play this game with a dog that is too big to run through your legs. That is definitely not a good idea! If your dog is very big, play the Chase Game instead – it teaches the building of acceleration and is still lots of fun!

3. The Whirlwind – Building Proximity

There are situations in life when you need to get hold of your dog after a recall. Some dogs follow their guardian's recall but instead of coming in close, they stop at an arm's length away from their human because they don't want to go back on the leash. The Whirlwind teaches your dog the concept that coming in close to you is super fun and worthwhile.

The Protocol:
- Toss your dog a freebie using a bowling movement (you're getting pretty good at this now, right?).
- Wait for your dog to find and eat the treat. The moment your dog is about to turn around to ask for more, give your check-in cue, followed by your anchor cue.
- Repeat the anchor cue until your dog is with you. While your dog is still running towards you, show them another treat in your outstretched hand, turn with the hand outstretched and lead them 360° around you. Throw the treat in the direction your dog came from.
- Wait for your dog to find and eat the treat. The moment your dog is about to turn around to ask for more, give your check-in cue, followed by your anchor cue again.
- Repeat several times. Lead your dog around you and throw out the treats five to ten times.
- Don't forget to cool your dog down by fading the energy from your toss, then give a treat from your hand and sprinkle some more treats on the ground before you move on.

Isla Playing the Whirlwind.

Isla Playing the Whirlwind.

4. Ping-pong – They Listen To Me But Never To My Partner

The Ping-pong Game teaches your dog that listening to all the members of your family is super fun and worthwhile. You can even play this game when introducing a new person to your dog, such as a dog walker or someone who looks after your dog while you are on holiday.

Some dogs will only listen to the recall of the one person in the household who spends the most time with them or does most of the training or husbandry. They might completely ignore the other family members. It's easy to see that this can be frustrating for others who might harbour bad feelings towards the dog because they seemingly love one family member more than others; it might even lead to fights and quarrels between partners or siblings.

The Protocol:

- This exercise needs at least two people to be present – it works best when there are several people. Each player should be well-armed with yummy treats.
- Feed your dog a couple of freebies from your hand. Stop feeding and show your dog your empty hand.
- This is the signal for the second person to recall the dog by using the check-in cue, followed by the anchor cue until the dog is with the second person who called.
- The second person feeds a couple of treats from their hand. They stop feeding and show the dog the empty hand.
- This is the signal for the next person to call the dog by using the check-in cue, followed by the

anchor cue until the dog is with the person who called.

- Each person takes turns calling the dog to them.
- Don't forget to cool your dog down by fading the energy from your toss, then give a treat from your hand and sprinkle some more treats on the ground before you move on.

Troubleshooting:

If your dog finds it difficult to tear themself away from one player, show them your empty hands again. The calling player decreases distance between themself and the dog and keeps repeating the anchor cue until the dog realises what to do. They can use a high pitched voice and body movement away from the dog to make it easier for the dog to follow.

5. Playing Catch – Building Proximity

Playing Catch or Tag is another game to build a concept of proximity in your dog. Playing this game requires your dog to come in close to you. You can play it around any obstacle, such as park benches, trees or even your garden shed. It's so much fun but be careful not to hurt yourself.

The Protocol:

- Toss your dog a freebie.
- Wait for your dog to find and eat the treat. The moment they are about to turn around to ask for more, give your check-in cue and start running around the obstacle. If you have enough breath, give your anchor cue until your dog catches up with you.
- When your dog catches up with you, reward them with a treat from your hand and toss another treat to the ground.
- Wait for your dog to find and eat the treat. The moment your dog is about to turn around to

ask for more, give your check-in cue and start running around the obstacle again.
- Repeat several times.
- Try to be unpredictable and change direction frequently.
- Don't forget to cool your dog down by fading the energy from your toss, then give a treat from your hand and sprinkle some more treats on the ground before you move on.

6. Hide and Seek – Out Of Sight But Not Out Of Mind

Playing Hide and Seek teaches your dog that your recall counts even if you are out of sight.

For this game you need an area with several hides – trees, bushes, garden sheds, that kind of thing - and a helper to hold your dog while you hide.

The Protocol:
- Ask your helper to hold your dog on a well-fitted harness while you hide.
- Call your dog using your check-in cue and then your anchor cue.
- Repeat the anchor cue so that your dog can follow your voice until they find you. Reward them with several yummy treats from your hand.
- Now hold your dog on their harness while the other person hides.
- Take turns hiding and calling your dog using the check-in cue, followed by the anchor cue.
- Don't forget to cool your dog down by fading the energy from your toss, then give a treat from your hand and sprinkle some more treats on the ground before you move on.

Important:

This should be fun for you and your dog! So please don't play this game if your dog suffers from separation anxiety or shows severe signs of stress as soon as you are out of sight! If anyone's ever told you to hide from your dog when they ignore you on your walks, please don't do it. This is bad advice! By hiding, your very confident and independent dog will learn that they, indeed, don't need you and they can reward themself in the environment. On the flip side, a fearful and insecure dog will lose their trust in you as their guardian. On their walks, your dog should be able to delve into and get lost in their dog world of scents. They need to sniff to gather information about their environment and release stress. If you punish them for taking their me-time by hiding out of sight, they will panic. Feeling insecure makes a dog more attentive to their owner – that's a fact. -But don't mistake a clingy, fearful dog for a happy and confident dog who wants to be with you!

7. The Fake Leash

The Fake leash teaches your dog that being close to you is the best place in the world. Some dogs try to get away from their guardians as fast as they can. As soon as they hear their leash being unclipped they've sprinted to the other end of the park. When called, they stop an arm's length away from their human because if they get any closer, they worry about being grabbed and put back on their leash.

The Protocol:
Stage 1: Fake to unleash your dog
- Put your dog on a double leash and unclip one of the two carabiners. As soon as your dog hears the click of the carabiner, it's party time! Throw some treats, run with your dog, pull out a tug, do whatever your dog loves!

- Play the fake leash whenever you unleash your dog.

Stage 2: Fake to put your dog on a leash

- Do you remember the 10:1 rule? For every time that grabbing your dog's harness or collar has a negative consequence (lie leash on or end of the playtime with their dog buddy), you need ten positive consequences to make up for this aversive experience.
- Call your dog when nothing exciting is happening.
- Use your check-in cue, followed by your anchor cue.
- As soon as your dog is with you, grab your dog's harness or collar, give them a yummy treat, and immediately release them and send them off to play again!

Nanook playing the Fake Leash.

8. All Eyes On Me! – Topping Up Your Dog's Check-in Cue

Making eye contact with your dog is the basis for any communication. Many dogs couldn't care less about their owners when they're out and about. There's way too much fun to be had! By reinforcing eye contact, your dog will actively look at you more often in the future.

Remember that 90% of your recall depends on your dog's reorientation? This is why this game is super important! Play it in various situations. Start in a low distraction environment and work through your list of distractions. Up your game until your dog is able to check-in with you in a busy street, next to a school yard or a flock of livestock (always on leash!)

The Protocol:
- Count ten treats into your treat bag. Toss your dog a freebie treat to your left and wait for them to find and eat the treat. The moment your dog turns around and looks up at you for more, give your check-in cue and drop the next treat on the ground to your right. Repeat until all treats are gone.

Nanook playing All Eyes on Me.

Part 4: Go-Pro Games - Taking Your Double Recall To The Next Level

The Equipment

After your dog has successfully mastered the Double Recall Games in part three, it's time to go pro!

To play the following Go-Pro Games you will need a toy that your dog loves! I recommend the use of a so-called snack dummy or prey dummy, but any fun toy will do.

Wondering what a prey dummy is? If you've never come across one before, a prey dummy is a toy that was developed for gun dog training. It looks like a pencil case with a zipper and is stuffed with treats. Some prey dummies are made of rabbit fur, sheepskin or fake fur for added authenticity. Dogs love them - especially when they bite into the fur (the prey) – and it skyrockets their motivation to earn more rewards.

Feeding your dog from the prey dummy leads to the release of endorphins which will calm the dog down. But don't think you can get away with giving your dog a boring treat from the prey dummy. Instead, let them stick their nose into the prey dummy and enjoy the feeling of consuming their prey. Another perk of using a prey dummy is that you are the only one who can open the zipper and give your dog access to the treats inside. Successful training is teamwork! In playing with the prey dummy, your dog will quickly learn that coming back to you is beneficial because you will give them access to their reward.

If you're looking to buy a fur prey dummy online, check out the link at the back of this book. Moreover, you will need a flirt pole, several toys, such as a frisbee, a tug, a ball on a string etc. and versatile, high value treats, such as spray cheese or squeezy cheese, hot dogs, meatballs etc.

Use a three to five-meter leash or a ten-meter long line, attached to a well-fitted harness. Retractable leads and those shorter than two meters are not suitable for these games.

Distractions Will Only Be Distractions Until They Become Reinforcers!

A clever way to train a Rocket Recall is to use the Premack Principle. Never heard of it? Let me explain. US biologist Richard B. Premack discovered that a more probable behaviour will reinforce a less probable behaviour. A more probable behaviour is either intrinsically motivated, (i.e. the behaviour in itself gives the dog pleasure) or it has been positively reinforced so often that the dog likes to do it. In other words, it's Granny's Law: "If you eat your vegetables, you can have your dessert".

Revisit your dog's list of distractions and mark all those that are safe for your dog to perform and that you can use as rewards.

MY DOG NANOOK'S LIST OF DISTRACTIONS

What does Nanook find hard to disengage from?

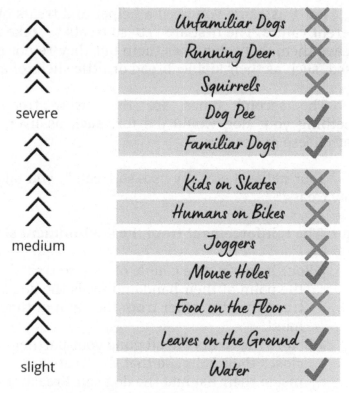

severe

medium

slight

Unfamiliar Dogs	✗
Running Deer	✗
Squirrels	✗
Dog Pee	✓
Familiar Dogs	✓
Kids on Skates	✗
Humans on Bikes	✗
Joggers	✗
Mouse Holes	✓
Food on the Floor	✗
Leaves on the Ground	✓
Water	✓

✓ Safe to perform. Can be used as environemtal rewards.

✗ Unsafe to perform. Cannot be used as rewards.

1. Go-Pro: You Can Have Your Cake And Eat It, Too!

Your dog will learn that moving away from a tempting stimulus in the environment is worthwhile, even if the distraction is ongoing.

For this game you need a helper and treats of two different values. The first are "so-so treats" – take them or leave them. Your dog likes them but they're not really fussed, such as their kibble, bread or little slices of apple.

The second types are the "wow treats" – something your dog would die for, such as liver pate, spray cheese or hot dog.

Your helper takes the "so-so treats", you take the "wow treats".

Step 1: The reinforcement from the environment stops

- Your helper puts a couple of "so-so treats" onto the palm of their hand and feeds the dog one treat after the other from the palm of their hand.
- Before the treats are all gone your partner stops, closes their palm, so that the treats are now inside their fist and the dog can't reach them.
- You now call your dog using the Double Recall. Even if your dog doesn't react immediately, go on anchoring until they are with you.
- Feed your dog the "wow treats" from your hand. To make it a double reinforcement, you can now send the dog back to your helper who opens their fist and feeds the dog. Now the dog has their "wow-treats" with you, and the "so-so treats" on top of that.

Step 2: The reinforcement from the environment is ongoing

- Your helper puts a couple of "so-so treats" onto the palm of their hand and feeds the dog one treat after the other from the palm of their hand.
- This time the helper doesn't stop feeding to make a fist, but he goes on feeding. However, they feed the dog slowly with longer pauses in between the treats.
- You now call your dog using the Double Recall. If your dog doesn't react immediately, go on anchoring until they are with you.
- Feed your dog the "wow treats" from your hand. To make it a double reinforcement, you can now send the dog back to your helper who feeds the dog, so that they can have both: the "wow-treats" with you, and the "so-so treats" on top of that.

Nanook playing "You can have your Cake and eat it, too!"

2. Go-Pro: The Triangle Of Success

The Triangle of Success is all about cooperation between you and your dog; keeping a clear mind, even when surrounded by strong distractions, and impulse control. It derives from gun dog training and here's the deal: if your dog comes back to you, then you allow them to run where they wanted to go before you called them back!

Imagine a triangle that consists of you, your dog and the prey dummy that you put out. Your dog wants that prey dummy so much! Under normal circumstances, they would run straight to the prey dummy. Instead, you ask them to come back to you and then you release them to the prey dummy as soon as they are with you.

Please note here: you do not need to feed your dog for coming back because by sending them to the prey dummy you're giving them what they want. And that's the best reinforcement possible!

The Protocol:
Step 1: The basic triangle
- Ask your dog to sit and stay or ask a helper to hold your dog.
- Put out a toy or a prey dummy, stuffed with treats.
- Start with a short distance between you and your dog and a longer distance between your dog and the prey dummy. This will make it easier for your dog in step 1.
- Recall your dog using the Double Recall. Give your check-in cue, followed by your anchor cue. Repeat the anchor cue until your dog is with you.
- The moment they are with you, immediately send them off to get their prey dummy with a

releasing hand gesture and an encouraging "go get it!"
- Run over to the prey dummy together with your dog and open the prey dummy up together.
- Let your dog eat out of the prey dummy and have a game of tug.

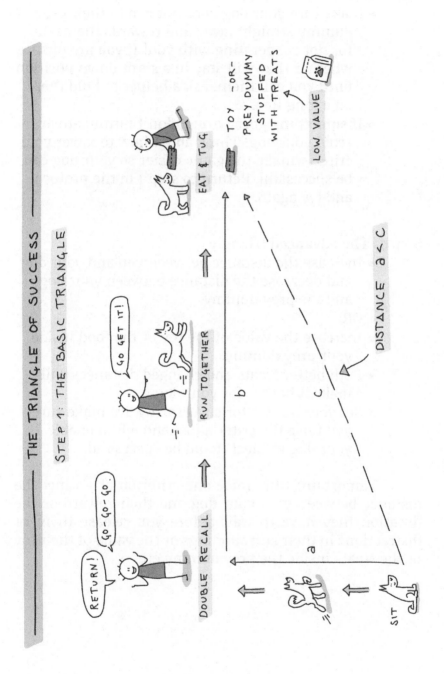

THE TRIANGLE OF SUCCESS

STEP 1: THE BASIC TRIANGLE

RETURN!
GO-GO-GO.

GO GET IT!

EAT & TUG

TOY -OR-
PREY DUMMY
STUFFED
WITH TREATS

LOW VALUE

DOUBLE RECALL

RUN TOGETHER

b

a

c

SIT

DISTANCE a < c

Important:
- Make sure your dog does not run to their prey dummy straight away and rewards themself for not cooperating with you! If you are unsure whether they will stay in a sit or down position until you call them, ask a helper to hold them on a long line.
- If something goes wrong, don't intimidate or scold your dog! Think about how to lower your criteria/make the game easier so your dog can be successful. Return to step 1 in the protocol and try again.

Step 2: The advanced triangle
- Increase the distance between you and your dog and decrease the distance between your dog and the prey dummy.
- OR
- Increase the value of the toy or the food inside your prey dummy.
- Both better treats and changed distances will make it harder for your dog.
- Set your dog up for success. Always make sure you raise the criteria just enough to enable your dog to meet it and be successful.

Important: Only raise one criterion at a time: the distance between you, your dog and their reward or the duration they have to wait before you release them or distractions in their surroundings or the value of their toy or the treats inside the prey dummy etc.

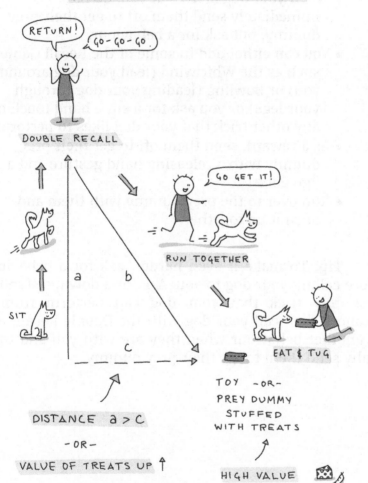

THE TRIANGLE OF SUCCESS

STEP 2: THE ADVANCED TRIANGLE

RETURN!

GO-GO-GO

DOUBLE RECALL

GO GET IT!

RUN TOGETHER

SIT

a

b

c

EAT & TUG

TOY -OR-
PREY DUMMY
STUFFED
WITH TREATS

DISTANCE a > c

-OR-

VALUE OF TREATS UP ↑

HIGH VALUE

1 CRITERION AT A TIME!

Step 3: Asking for a behaviour

- Put out a toy or a prey dummy, stuffed with treats.
- Recall your dog using the Double Recall. Give your check-in cue, followed by the anchor cue until your dog is with you.
- When your dog arrives at you, do not immediately send them off to get their prey dummy, but ask for a behaviour.
- You can either add in some of the Recall Games, such as the Whirlwind (lead your dog around you) or Bowling (leading your dog through your legs) or you ask for a sit, a hand touch or any other trick that your dog likes to perform.
- As a reward, send them off to get their prey dummy with a releasing hand gesture and a "go get it!"
- Run over to the prey dummy with them and open it up together.

Tip: To make it even harder, ask for a behaviour before calling your dog to you. Ask for a down, a stand, a twist, any trick that your dog can perform from a distance. Then call your dog with the Double Recall, ask for another behaviour when they are with you and then finally send them to get their prey dummy.

Simone Mueller

Nanook Playing the Triangle of Success.

**Before releasing him to the prey dummy,
I ask him to perform a hand touch.**

Step 4: Distractions become live rewards

- Remember the Premack Principle? Go back to your list of safe distractions that have now become rewards from the environment.
  Of course, you cannot allow your dog to chase wildlife or cars and it's impossible to send them to every single dog they want to meet. But some distractions are safe to use, such as swimming, digging, sniffing, meeting a buddy etc.
- Imagine a triangle in which these live rewards take the place of your prey dummy.
- Lower the criteria again and increase the distance between your dog and the live reward, while at the same time you decrease the distance between you and your dog.
- Use the Double Recall to call your dog and immediately send them to their live reward.
- Go through all your distractions that are safe to perform and for every single one carefully raise criteria as described in steps 2 and 3.
- Use your imagination to create new challenges for yourself and your dog.

Keep in mind that impulse control is limited, so do not overtrain. Play for three to five minutes, then take a break and let your dog be a dog again.

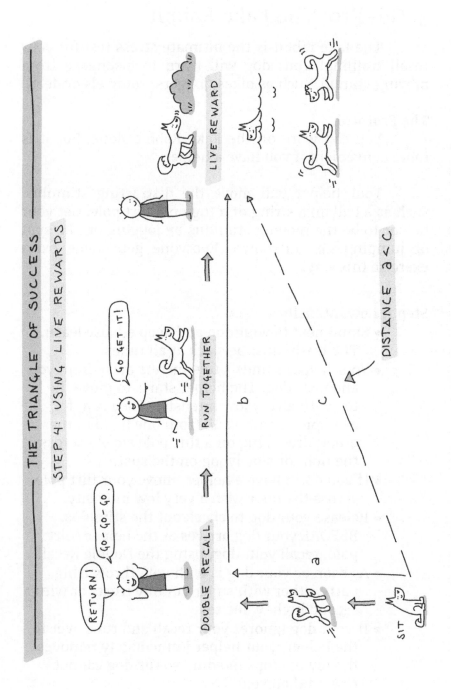

3. Go-Pro: The Fake Rabbit

The fake rabbit is the ultimate stress test for your recall training! Your dog will learn to disengage from moving stimuli, such as bikes, joggers, squirrels or deer.

The Protocol:

You can work on the Fake Rabbit alone, but it is more convenient if you have a helper.

Your helper will move the distracting stimulus, such as a ball on a string or a tug on a flirt pole. Get your helper to be the moving stimulus by jogging on the spot or jumping up and down. Everyone gets some extra exercise this way!

Step 1: Low intensity
- Stand next to your dog and keep a loose leash. The leash must be slack at all times!
- Your helper stands 3 to 5 meters away from you and your dog. The helper starts to move the toy with a very low intensity. They can, for example, throw a ball from one hand to the other, drag a tug on a flirt pole slowly across the floor or slowly jog on the spot.
- If you don't have a helper, move your flirt pole across the floor with a very low intensity.
- Release your dog to check out the stimulus. BEFORE your dog arrives at the helper /flirt pole, recall your dog, using the Double Recall.
- As soon as your dog is with you, throw a big party either with super yummy treats or with a second high-value toy.
- If your dog ignores your recall and runs over to the helper, your helper immediately removes the toy or stops moving, so the dog cannot reward themself.

- If this happens more than once, lower the intensity of the moving stimulus and repeat several times on a level that your dog can manage.

Step 2: Moderate intensity
- Stand next to your dog and make sure the leash is slack.
- Your helper stands 3 to 5 meters away from you and your dog and starts to move the toy with a medium intensity. They can, for example, throw a ball into the grass, drag a tug on a flirt pole across the floor or jog on the spot.
- If you don't have a helper, move your flirt pole across the floor with a medium intensity.
- Release your dog to check out the stimulus. BEFORE your dog arrives at the helper / flirt pole, recall your dog, using the Double Recall.
- As soon as your dog is with you, throw a big party either with super yummy treats or with a second high-value toy.

Step 3: High intensity
- Stand next to your dog and make sure the leash is slack.
- Your helper is standing 3 to 5 meters away from you and your dog and starts to move the toy with a high intensity. They can, for example, throw a ball across the floor, wildly drag a tug on a flirt pole across the floor, or energetically jog on the spot or jump up and down.
- If you don't have a helper, move your flirt pole across the floor with a high intensity.
- Release your dog to check out the stimulus. BEFORE your dog arrives at the helper / flirt pole, recall your dog, using the Double Recall.

- As soon as your dog is with you, throw a big party either with super yummy treats or with a second high-value toy.

Isla playing the Fake Rabbit.

Step 4: Upping the criteria
Always work on one criterion at a time! Either distance or duration or distraction. Make sure the leash is slack at all times!

- Stand further away from your dog, so your dog is closer to the helper.
- Let your dog run further away from you before you call them.
- Let your dog chase the tug on a flirt pole longer before you call them back.
- Throw a ball yourself and recall your dog.
- Have your helper jog up from behind and pass you and your dog from behind.
- Throw a higher value toy, such as a frisbee.

- Repeatedly throw a ball but do not recall your dog every time. Sometimes they can chase it, sometimes they can't. Be unpredictable!

Important!

If you work with your dog on a leash, always make sure the leash is slack! If your dog learns they will be stopped by a leash before reacting to your recall, the recall will never work off-leash in real-life situations.

Always do this exercise on a well-fitted harness, not a collar. If your dog runs into the leash wearing a collar, they might injure their neck and spine.

And If They Don't Come Back?

The more distractions you add into your training, the bigger the risk that your recall will go wrong from time to time.

What can you do after a recall–fail during training?

If your dog is on a leash:

- Are you sure your dog heard the check-in cue? Sometimes dogs are too distracted or the environment is too noisy.
- If you're sure they heard your check-in cue but ignored it... breathe in and out! It is only fair to give them one or two seconds to let the check-in cue sink in into their dog world.
- If your dog chooses check-in with you in the meantime, then start giving your anchor cue!
- If they still don't react, take on the leash to prevent them from moving further away from you and rewarding themself for ignoring you.
- As soon as the leash is tight, wait for a second. Do they check-in with you now? Then start

giving your anchor cue and reward as soon as they are with you.

- If they still don't react, step sideways into your dog's peripheral vision, move your hand and address your dog by their name or make a kissy noise. When they turn towards you, mark and move backwards while giving your anchor cue. Reward as soon as they are with you.
- If they're over threshold and not able to respond to any of these measures, as a last resort, grab their harness and guide them out of the situation.

What can you do after a recall-fail in a real-life situation?

If your dog is off-leash and running away from you even after you used the Double Recall:

- Stay calm and count to five. Try again.
- If they come back now, throw a big party, even though they didn't react immediately. It is still a great achievement that they chose to turn away from a strong trigger in the environment.
- Never scold your dog for coming back!!
- If they still don't react and are running further and further away from you, start anchoring slowly and steadily. The old rule that a "command is only given once" does not apply for the anchor cue! Continue to repeat your anchor cue, even if they keep running away from you or are out of sight. Remember the troubleshooting advice from earlier? When your dog is in chasing mode, the thinking part of their brain (the part that's responsible for listening to your cue) is switched off and they

cannot hear you. Yet, at some point, your dog will need to refocus and orient themself. This is when your anchor cue kicks in and your dog will come back to you.

- When they are on their way back to you, maintain a friendly voice and an inviting body language, even if you are boiling with anger inside. If you let them feel your anger, your dog is likely to slow down to appease you and be reluctant to come back to you after the next chase.
- When they are close to you, scatter some treats on the floor and put them on a leash while they're searching for the treats.
- Increase the frequency and intensity of your recall training for the next ten days.

The End Of The Book – The Beginning Of Your Training Journey!

Recall training is a work in progress. It's a never-ending story and a challenge for every dog guardian's creativity. The Double Recall is not a magic wand. You cannot wave it and your dog will magically stop in their tracks and fly back to you. A recall is always an aversive event and goes against what the dog wants to do at that moment. We are constantly competing with the environment and sometimes those distractions can be so exciting for your dog. So never stop training your double recall, playing recall games and rewarding each recall heavily.

Yet, a Rocket Recall can become reality. You and your dog can achieve it through persistence, hard work and clever training.

Instead of seeing your dog's recall as a struggle, turn your training into an endless opportunity to build a super-strong bond between you and your dog by playing games that will set you both up for success!

This training program has provided you with all the necessary tools you will need to successfully scaffold a Rocket Recall without using intimidation, pain or fear.

In this training program you:

- became familiar with the Double Recall, a tool that gives your dog the support they need to fly back to you, even past the strongest distractions.

- learned how to train the Double Recall step-by-step with a word cue and a whistle.
- discovered functional and need-oriented reinforcers to reward your dog.
- became aware of the typical mistakes that can spoil your success.
- learned fun recall games from basic to pro-level that will cement your dog's Rocket Recall.
- became empowered to successfully and independently continue training long after finishing this training program.

Whether you use purely positive training with your dog or a balanced approach and you're searching for ways to reduce punishment, give this program a go and you will be amazed at how far motivation-based and need-oriented training will take you and your best four-legged friend!

Ready – Steady – Go – Recall!

Acknowledgements

This book would not have been possible without my amazing trainer colleagues:

- Claire Staines from Lothlorien Dog Services in Scotland, my dear friend and mentor from whom I was allowed to learn, and through whom I still keep on learning. Claire, you are an inspiration!
- Lhanna Dickson for putting time and thoughts into this protocol. Thank you for your precious opinion and feedback!
- A big shout out to the whole Lothlorien Team for your ongoing support and for making me feel close to you, even though I'm actually quite far away.

Special Thank Yous Go Out To:

- Sonja Rupp, for the lovely photos of my dogs.
- Michelle Mäder and Andrea Pfander for the cover photo of little Johnny, showing off his Rocket Recall.
- Michelle Emerson and Charlotte Garner for giving my text a good polish.
- Päivi Kokko for contributing the amazing sketches.

I want to mention at least some of the colleagues that paved the way for force-free, science-based training protocols that I refer to in this training program:

- Dr. Ute Blaschke Berthold, a visionary trainer, and behaviourist who developed the Double Recall.
- Patricia B. McConnell Ph.D: "Acoustic structure and receiver response in mammalian signal systems"
- Leslie Nelson: "Really Reliable Recall – Easy to follow steps to train your dog to come to you when it really counts".
- Sonja Meiburg and her fabulous recall book „Raketenstart Rückruf – Sicher Abrufen leicht gemacht".
- Anja Fiedler, who merged and perfected several Predation Substitute Training protocols in her comprehensive training program "Jagdverhalten – verstehen, kontrollieren, ausgleichen". If you read German, this is a must-read!
- Grisha Steward, whose book and training program BAT 2.0 heavily influenced the leash handling in my books. BAT 2.0 is the best resource out there if you're looking for a mindful way to handle your dog.

The biggest thank you is to my husband Kai for his ongoing support, his patience, and for always listening to me going on about dogs and training.

Last but not least, this book is dedicated to my dogs Malinka, Nanook, and Isla, my best teachers and closest companions.

About the Author

Simone Mueller, MA is a certified dog trainer and dog behavior consultant (ATN) from Germany.

She specializes in force-free anti-predation training and is the author of the Predation Substitute Training™ series: "Hunting Together", "Rocket Recall" and "Don't Eat That".

Simone is proud to be an Associate Trainer at the Scotland-based Lothlorien Dog Training Club (AT-LDTC) and a member of The Initiative of Force-Free Dog Training, the Pet Professional Guild (PPG) and the Pet Dog Trainers of Europe (PDTE).

Learn more at: http://www.predation-substitute-training.com

Follow Simone's work on Facebook and Instagram:
facebook.com/predationsubstitutetraining
instagram.com/predation_substitute_training
#predationsubstitutetraining

One Final Note

If, after reading and following this training program you feel like Rocket Recall will never work for your dog, write me an email! Yes, I'm entirely serious - humans need to learn and adapt just as much as their canine companions and your take on the results will help me refine my approach(es) for the future.

If, on the other hand, you liked this training program and think that this is a game-changer in the relationship with your dog, please let the world know by leaving a rating and review on Amazon!

I ask this because reviews are the lifeblood of any independent book on Amazon. Without stars and reviews, there's a better-than-average chance you wouldn't have found this training program in the first place. Please take thirty seconds of your time (or potentially even less than that!) to support me as an independent author by leaving a rating.

If you would click five stars after the last page on your Kindle device or leave a positive review on Amazon, I would deeply appreciate it.

Click Account & Lists in the upper right corner -> Your Account -> Orders -> scroll down your orders and then click the Write a Product Review button on the right.

It's a bit hidden, but by doing this, your review will be a "Verified Purchase", and this carries far more weight.

After all, a quick rating or review helps me to provide my dogs with more toys and treats and honestly, which dog in the world doesn't deserve more toys and treats?

Thank you very much!
Best wishes for you and your dog
Simone

Your Training Plan for a Rocket Recall

To download the whole training log as a free, printable PDF from my website, follow the link: http://www.predation-substitute-training.com/rocketrecalltraininglog

Or scan the QR code:

The Parts of the Predation Substitute Training™ Puzzle

ROCKET RECALL

FOR DOGS WHO
LOVE TO CHASE

FOR DOGS WHO
LOVE TO SCAVENGE

HUNTING TOGETHER

DON'T EAT THAT!

Now that you have progressed through the protocol of the Rocket Recall, it's time to use your newfound skills and tools to further build on your relationship with your dog.

Is Hunting your dog's favourite hobby? – Go "Hunting Together"

For dogs that love to hunt, teaching them a Rocket Recall is just one component of the holistic approach that forms PST. Understanding and implementing the entire Predation Substitute Training protocol will help you achieve better, longer-lasting results.

If your dog is always on the look-out for rabbits, deer, birds, or any other wild animals, and won't think twice about disappearing into the distance to chase them, then I recommend you look at the other book in my Predation Substitute Training Series: Hunting Together.

Hunting Together will help to give you a deeper understanding of the reasons behind your dog's hunting behaviour, as well as successful ways to manage this effectively.

Would you like a reading sample?

Then turn the page and discover a new perspective on your dog's predatory behaviour and even see your dog's hunting skills through different eyes.

Hunting Together

What Is Predation Substitute Training?

The term "Predation Substitute Training" (PST) has a double meaning. It implies that, through playing Predation Substitute Games with your dog, you'll be able to redirect predatory urges into a harmless owner-centric game, ensuring that predatory energy is released in a safe and controlled way.

The real game-changer, however, is in the deeper meaning of the term. Predation Substitute Training equips you with Predation Substitute Tools. Instead of interrupting your dog's predatory behaviour and ending the fun, you train your dog to perform a safe part to the predatory sequence instead of an unsafe part. E.g. instead of letting them chase, you let them stalk wildlife. This will still let them do what they want to do. In short, hunt!

I have been successfully using this protocol for several years now. Nanook, my 10-year-old Australian Shepherd, used to be a big chaser. Through PST, he has become a passionate visual stalker. Rather than physically taking chase, he's now able to happily sit down and visually follow a running deer in the field while staying by my side.

While it's worked out very well for both my own dogs and my clients' dogs, I want to stress something important before we get too deep into practice and theory. Predation Substitute Training is not a quick fix that will stop your dog from chasing. Like most proven dog training techniques, it's hard work and will require a lot of effort to put into your everyday walks to introduce and reinforce concepts. That being said, the positive outcomes that grow from this fair, motivation-centred and need-oriented training are amazing. Once PST has been successfully implemented, your dog will be more controllable in the presence of wildlife. They will be more likely to react to your recall, sharing the joy of performing safe parts of the predatory sequence with you.

Make no mistake about it: predation is pure happiness for our dogs! Imagine using that feeling of pleasure, fulfillment and motivation that our dogs find in predation to enforce useful training and deepen your bond with your dog. It's not only possible, it's a smart move!

In this training program, you'll find all of the training techniques and tools that you'll need to successfully harness your dog's predatory instincts - all without using intimidation, pain or fear:

- You will understand what predation is and why your dog loves hunting so much.
- You will have Predation Substitute Tools at hand to functionally reinforce your dog, allowing them to stop and control themselves instead of chasing after game.
- You will be equipped with several need-oriented Predation Substitute Games to create a safe outlet for your dog's predatory energy.
- And you will be provided with a safety net to interrupt unwanted predatory chasing with an emergency cue.

All I ask from you is that you keep an open mind while learning this motivation-centred, science-based approach, and (of course) that you have fun with your dog.

So grab your treat pouch, stuff it with delicious dog treats, and dig out your dog's most exciting toys. It's time to get started!

Hunting Together by Simone Mueller is available as e-book (ISBN 978-3-9821878-7-7), paperback (ISBN 978-3-9821878-6-0) and hardcover (ISBN 979-8393241285).

Do you have a "Hoover Dog"?

If you have a dog who loves to scavenge and you want to learn how to manage this successfully without using force or aversive methods. 'Don't Eat That!' is full of useful information about how to keep your dog safe by stopping them from scavenging and eating food they find on the ground. As you will discover, this is done by providing your dog with suitable scavenging outlets, instead of trying to eliminate this behaviour from their life entirely. This approach provides you with much more sustainable results than you would be able to achieve if you tried to stop your dog from showing this behaviour completely.

Are you curious why dogs love to scavenge? Here's a reading sample!

Don't Eat That

Why Do Dogs Love To Scavenge?

The fact you are reading this book means there is a high chance that you already know that dogs love to scavenge! But you might be surprised to learn that there are several deep-rooted reasons for this; it's not as simple as them just feeling hungry or being greedy! Understanding why your dog loves scavenging so much can help you better work out how to manage this behavior successfully.

So, here are the reasons why your dog values scavenging so highly:

Scavenging Is A Basic Need For Your Dog

Something that every species of living beings rely upon is finding food. This is essential to their survival and is no different for our dogs. Although our domesticated pet dogs no longer rely on scavenging as their only way of finding food, it is often still something they naturally desire and feel the need to do.

Your Dog Is Simply Hungry

This is perhaps the most common reason which comes to mind when owners are faced with a scavenging dog! Many think their dog is doing it to be greedy, but in actual fact, they may be hungry. Some modern-day dog foods don't satisfy your dog's hunger for long, so when they come across something tasty on the ground, it can be tough for them to resist, even if it's something potentially harmful to them. Consider the type and amount of food your dog is getting, and how often they are fed over the day. Making changes to these things can be a good starting point for reducing your dog's scavenging, although it won't eliminate it completely! Even dogs who are fed high-quality foods can still find the temptation of some 'freebies' too difficult to ignore! Try feeding your dog a handful of food around 20 minutes before you go for a walk. Do this for a week and see if this can reduce their scavenging urges.

Dogs Find Scavenging Intrinsically Reinforcing

There are two things at play here that make scavenging intrinsically reinforcing for our dogs - their seeking and play systems. The seeking system is the most addictive of the two and can be likened to people who enjoy gambling. Although they don't win every time they take part, the thrill of the possibility of winning keeps them coming back for more again and again. They invest increasing amounts of time, energy, and concentration in anticipation of a win that might happen, in exactly the same way a human would when playing on slot machines or placing bets. When your dog wins by finding something to eat on the floor, the feeling of euphoria and excitement, along with the Dopamine that is released into their system, makes them want to scavenge again.

The play system means that scavenging feels good for your dog, they enjoy it, and it makes them happy! Your dog's enjoying the searching, finding, sniffing, chewing, licking, eating, and swallowing aspects of scavenging food. This releases feel-good endorphins into your dog's system, leaving them happy, satisfied, and relaxed. It's not hard to see why they would want to repeat this process as often as possible so that they can feel this way more often! This is similar to how humans feel when we have a lavish 3-course meal. We feel indulged and will look forward to the next opportunity we have to experience this.

Scavenging Is Genetically Anchored Into Your Dog

Wolves first started spending time closer to humans because they realized there was food near them that was easily accessible. Humans created waste and stored food, which was much easier for the wolves to scavenge from than trying to hunt and kill their own food. This relationship turned out to be mutually beneficial as the wolves deterred other animals and intruders from getting too close to the humans. This sparked the start of evolution from wolves to the dogs we know and love today.

Some wild dogs still live in a very similar way to their ancestors, living on the outskirts of villages and scavenging from what the villagers leave behind. Some breeds still retain these strong instincts to scavenge, even though they no longer depend on it for their survival.

Your Dog Is Used To Needing To Scavenge

The saying 'old habits die hard' is relevant to dogs who have been used to needing to scavenge to survive. Dogs that have lived on the streets, often for several months, need to scavenge food to eat. This could be hunting and killing animals, or the easier route for them is scavenging food that humans leave behind. In fact, their whole life will have been structured around finding food, and it will have taken up a large part of each day for them. They will have practised their scavenging skills to make them excellent at finding things to eat, so they are not wasting precious time and energy searching for food. So, it can be tough for them to stop suddenly, even if their new lifestyle no longer requires them to do it.

Boredom Can Make Your Dog Scavenge More

This is particularly common in breeds with high intelligence and energy levels. If they're not provided with enough mental and physical stimulation, your dog may start using scavenging to remedy their boredom. This gives them something fun and rewarding to do. So, it's important to ensure your dog's mental and physical needs are met, before you start this training protocol. Without this, the training won't be as effective.

Over-aroused Dogs Tend To Scavenge More

Dogs that are stressed, anxious, or over-aroused can use scavenging as a way to distract themselves and make themselves feel better. Dogs that are reactive towards other animals, people, and new scenarios can be more likely to resort to scavenging to try and help them feel more in control and calmer. If you think that your dog is scavenging because of underlying stress, or to try and distract themselves from stressful situations, it's best to contact a force-free trainer or behaviorist for advice prior to starting this training protocol.

Your Dog Is Searching For A Novel Taste

Humans tend to be creatures of habit, and we like to stick with what we know. So often, once we find a food that suits our dog, we stick with the same flavor, day after day, month after month. Although this might be the most convenient option for us, it is by far the most boring option for our dogs! Unless they suffer from allergies or intolerances, our dogs can benefit from having a wide selection of different flavors and protein sources in their diet. Whether they are raw fed, kibble fed, or you cook at home for them, so long as their diets are complete, nutritious, and tasty for them, that is the main thing! It will quickly become monotonous if dogs constantly eat the same food for extended periods. This can lead to them having a stronger urge to scavenge in a desperate bid to find something different and more exciting to eat!

Artificial Selection Can Increase Scavenging

The artificial selection of certain breeds can increase the likelihood and frequency of their scavenging behavior. This is regularly shown in members of the hound family, who are bred to live and work in large packs of other hounds. Many working hounds live in a large group and are fed together, meaning it's in their best interest to find, grab and eat the food as quickly as possible, to make sure they get a decent amount. Those that are not as fast, will get little to no food and will be hungry, so it's beneficial for them to refine their scavenging skills to become more successful at it.

Also, some gundog breeds like the Labrador, Flat Coated Retriever, and Golden Retriever have been found to be missing part of or all of the gene known as POMC. The Proopiomelanocortin gene (POMC) gene affects appetite, food motivation, fat storage, and, most importantly, satiety. Satiety signals when your dog is full; without this signal working correctly, which is the case with dogs with the faulty POMC gene, they won't know that they feel full. So, they will continue to eat more, even though they have had enough! This can understandably increase their scavenging, as they constantly feel hungry, even if they are well-fed and nourished.

Your Dog May Have A Medical Condition

If your dog is an excessive scavenger, or has recently started scavenging much more than usual, it is best to get them checked thoroughly by your vet to rule out any potential medical issues before you begin training. If your dog's scavenging is due to a medical condition, then this training protocol won't be successful until your dog has received the appropriate treatment to cure or manage their condition effectively. Conditions like gastroenteritis, gastritis, heartburn, indigestion, pancreatitis, acid reflux, IBD, and parasites can all increase scavenging because your dog is looking for something to make themselves feel more comfortable or to ease their symptoms.

Pica Makes Your Dog Need To Scavenge

Pica is a disorder that makes your dog crave and eat non-food substances. This can mean pebbles, wood, plastic, paper, or anything else that is non-nutritional, wouldn't be considered as food, and holds no physical value to your dog. It is not fully understood what causes Pica. Some say it is a medical condition, related to stress and anxiety, because of boredom, or a habit the dog has formed. Whatever the reasoning behind the Pica, you should work with a qualified behaviorist under the advice of your veterinarian to try and manage it effectively before beginning this training protocol.

Don't Eat That by Simone Mueller is available as e-book (ISBN 978-3-9821878-5-3), paperback (ISBN 979-8359637954) and hardcover (ISBN 979-8368381244)

Made in the USA
Las Vegas, NV
29 January 2024

85042289R00066